*Letters to the Citizens
of the United States*

by Warren Bluhm

How to Play a Blue Guitar
A Bridge at Crossroads
Refuse to Be Afraid
A Scream of Consciousness
The Imaginary Bomb
The Imaginary Revolution
Myke Phoenix

edited by Warren Bluhm
Resistance to Civil Government
Letters to the Citizens of the United States
A Little Volume of Secrets
The Haunted Bookshop
Men in War
Trivia

Thomas Paine

Letters to the Citizens

of the United States

and Particularly to the Leaders
of the Federal Faction

edited and with introductory essays
by Warren Bluhm

warrenbluhm.com

Letters to the Citizens of the United States
by Thomas Paine
Introductory essays © 2009 Warren Bluhm
Edition 3.2 published December 2020
ISBN 978-1-0879-3692-5

What It Is

Thomas Paine, author of *Common Sense*, returned to the United States of America in 1802 after 15 years abroad. Upon his return he wrote a series of eight letters, seven of them in fairly quick succession, with his thoughts about revolution, liberty and the state of the young nation he helped create.

Who It Is

Warren Bluhm is an award-winning journalist and writer from Wisconsin who grew up a long time ago in a faraway land called New Jersey. When not writing and journaling, he lives quietly in a house in the woods with his life's mate and a variety of furry creatures.

The opening essays were first published in the blog "Montag ... and the clocks were striking thirteen" under the pseudonym B.W. Richardson.

Original content is licensed under the Creative Commons Attribution-Noncommercial-Share Alike License. To view a copy of this license, visit http://creativecommons.org/licenses/by-nc-sa/3.0/ or, (b) send a letter to Creative Commons, 171 2nd Street, Suite 300, San Francisco, California, 94105, USA. For more information visit www.creativecommons.org.

Introduction:
'peace, moderate taxes and mild government'

Being as woefully ignorant as most of my fellow citizens of the history of the country where I've spent all but a few days of my entire life, I was fascinated reading Thomas Paine's eight *Letters to the Citizens of the United States, and particularly to the leaders of the Federal faction*.

I was vaguely aware of the onerous Alien & Sedition Acts that were passed to suppress free speech, or more specifically the free speech of the Adams administration's political adversaries, but wasn't aware that some folks (like Paine) continued to call for investigation and prosecution of Adams for years after he left office — or that Adams snuck out of the White House early in the morning of March 4, 1800, not waiting to witness the inauguration of new president Thomas Jefferson.

And it seems that many debates we occasionally hear today already were raging when Paine wrote these epistles, in 1802 and 1803 (the eighth letter is dated 1805, but the first seven came in a November-to-April flurry).

Paine accuses Adams of wishing to dissolve the new republic and replace it with a monarchy-style system of succession much like Britain's, where the king's sons or daughters were destined to reign. (That may explain why John Quincy Adams later felt motivated to run for the office his father once held.) A Quasi-War against France was ginned up and Adams' Federalists clamored for the raising of an army of 50,000 men, ostensibly to defend against the inevitable French invasion. Paine felt this standing army was more likely to be used for some other, more sinister purpose.

> The suspicion against the late Administration is, that it was plotting to overturn the representative system of government, and that it spread alarms of invasions that had no foundation, as a pretence for raising and establishing a military force as the means of accomplishing that object ...

Of the Sedition Law, which levied a $2,000 fine and two years in prison for anyone who dared write or publish "any libel (without defining what a libel is) against the Government of the United States, or either House of Congress, or against the president ..."

> ... it is a much greater crime for a president to plot against a Constitution and the liberties of the people, than for an individual to plot against a President; and consequently, John Adams is accountable to the public for his conduct, as the individuals under his administration were to the sedition law.

> The object, however, of an enquiry, in this case, is not to punish, but to satisfy; and to shew, by example, to future administrations, that an abuse of power and trust, however disguised by appearances, or rendered plausible by pretence, is one time or other to be accounted for. (from letter VI)

Except for the changes in names and language use, Paine could have been writing after any recent administrations had been put to bed, for it appears the federalists eventually won the argument. It is now common "for a president to plot against a Constitution and the liberties of the people"and to keep the populace generally alarmed over the threat of invasion and all sorts of other alarming notions.

The Revolution had been fought to secure liberty and separate from the violent world and machinations of the British Empire.

> It requires only a prudent and honest administration to preserve America always at peace. Her distance from the European world frees her from its intrigues. But when men get into power, whose heads, like the head of John Adams, are filled with "strange notions" and counter revolutionary principles and projects, things will be sure to go wrong ...
>
> The independence of America would have added but little to her own happiness, and been of no benefit to the world, if her government had been formed on the corrupt models of the old world. It was the opportunity of beginning the world anew, as it were; and of bringing forward a new system of government in which the rights of all men should be preserved that gave value to independence. (from letter VIII; Paine's emphases)

It's fascinating to read the thoughts, 27 years later, of the man whose Common Sense framed the intellectual basis for cutting ties with old England, to see how he thought the young nation was fulfilling the dream. He clearly believed that the United States had dodged a bullet and that the election of Jefferson had preserved and re-established the principles of the Revolution.

> The characters of the late ad of the present Administrations are now sufficiently marked, and the adherents of each keep up the distinction. The former Administration rendered itself notorious by outrage, coxcombical parade, false alarms, a continual increase of taxes and an unceasing clamor for war; and as every vice has a virtue opposed to it the present Administration moves on the direct contrary line.

> The question, therefore, at elections is not properly a question upon persons, but upon principles. Those who are for peace, moderate taxes and mild government will vote for the Administration that conducts itself by those principles, in whatever hands that Administration might be. (from Letter VII)

Peace, moderate taxes and mild government continue to be ideals Americans believe in, judging from the campaign rhetoric that accompanies every election. Although Paine clearly believed Jefferson had delivered the goods in that respect, I can't think of a single modern president of whom the same could be said. Oh yes, peace and moderate taxes and mild government are promised — but the purpose of campaign rhetoric is to get elected, not to deliver the goods, especially not those particular goods.

If freedom were something granted by government, or a constitution, we would be in a heap of trouble. Fortunately we were born free. Governments can and often do obstruct freedom, but it is powerless to absolutely extinguish it. As long as liberty exists in a corner of a free man or woman's mind — and it always will — there's a glimmer of hope that common sense will prevail at last.

Warren Bluhm
August 4, 2009

'The little barkings of witless curs'

This morning I read carefully and joyously through Paine's first two letters, the joy a result of the encounter with an unapologetically free mind. Paine wrote to remind the citizens of the new United States of the principles behind their revolution 26 years earlier, and to call out the faction that he saw as turning back those principles in the name of "federalism."

One of Paine's observations gave me a small modicum of hope:

> There is in America, more than in any other country, a large body of people who attend quietly to their farms, or follow their several occupations; who pay no regard to the clamours of anonymous scribblers, who think for themselves, and judge of government, not by the fury of newspaper writers, but by the prudent frugality of its measures, and the encouragement it gives to the improvement and prosperity of the country; and who, acting on their own judgment, never come forward in an election but on some important occasion.
>
> When this body moves, all the little barkings of scribbling and witless curs pass for nothing.

Do these people still exist, and are they "a large body"? It's difficult to say, given the results of the last several elections — indeed, given the results of most elections — although much may be concluded by examining how many people don't participate in most elections.

Our days are filled with "little barkings of scribblings and witless curs" who advocate chains for all but their anointed rulers — scribblings, and their electronic equivalent in this modern age. Do those who think for themselves still exist in sufficient numbers to make a difference?

And by "make a difference," I mean nothing more than to make the witless curs and anointed ones irrelevant. Freedom means the ability to say, as the great fictional Independent Malcolm Reynolds (of the television show *Firefly* and the film *Serenity*) once said, "I got no need to beat you; I just want to go my way." Reynolds was a great example of Paine's people "who attend quietly to their farms, or to their several occupations."

Two hundred and seven years have passed since Paine wrote his letters, and the barkings have continued unceasingly. The embers of the flame he started with Common Sense still glow, often just barely.

The halls of government are filled with men and women anxious to extinguish those embers. They have grown fat and sassy on the backs of those willing to allow them to hold the reins of power; a little more Thomas Paine in our intellectual diets may be the cure.

Warren Bluhm
July 31, 2009

Delighting in serenity

Another gem from Letter III of Tom Paine's *Letters to the Citizens of the United States*, in which the great freedom advocate sounded the alarm about those who wanted to convert the US of A into an Old World monarchy/ dictatorship in 1802-03 (and later, some might say, succeeded beyond their wildest dreams):

> There is a general and striking difference between the genuine effects of truth itself, and the effects of falsehood believed to be truth. Truth is naturally benign; but false-hood believed to be truth is always furious. The former delights in serenity, is mild and persuasive, and seeks not the auxiliary aid of invention. The latter sticks at nothing.
>
> It has naturally no morals. Every lie is welcome that suits its purpose. It is the innate character of the thing to act in this manner, and the criterion by which it may be known, whether in politics or religion. When any thing is attempted to be supported by lying, it is presumptive evidence that the thing so supported is a lie also. The stock on which a lie can be grafted must be of the same species as the graft.

What's especially striking about Paine's letters is that, although the specific circumstances are different, the tactics of those who would assault individual freedoms haven't changed a whit. This is another example.

It seems to me that when you've touched on the basic truth of a thing, you experience the serenity Paine mentions. Any anxiety you might feel is more like an excitement of wanting or needing to share the truth. Truth does indeed have a "mild and persuasive" nature to it.

"Falsehood believed to be truth" is a different beast altogether. An intensity and even rage accompanies the demeanor of those who know they're right but maintain a sliver (or even a plank or two) of doubt. In its extreme, this is the anger of "We gotta round up them illegals and ship 'em back to Mexico before they finish ruinin' our country" or "That smoker over there in the corner is poisoning my air" and "The fight against climate change requires you to submit to the state, and how can you even doubt?"

Self-evident truth settles into the heart and takes up residence. Falsehood believed to be truth is the proverbial resounding gong or clanging cymbal. Again, it's Malcolm Reynolds and "I got no need to beat you; I just want to go my way."

The holder of truth knows that at some point, the truth will become self-evident even to the hardest to convince. The holder of the falsehood-believed-to-be-truth needs to convince, because maybe if he can find enough other people to believe the falsehood it really will be true. But a falsehood believed to be true by a vast majority is still false; that's the underlying frustration and the root of the fervor.

The truth "delights in serenity." What a wonderful phrase!

Warren Bluhm
August 1, 2009

*Letters to the Citizens
of the United States*

I.

from *The National Intelligencer*, November 15, 1802

After an absence of almost fifteen years, I am again returned to the country in whose dangers I bore my share, and to whose greatness I contributed my part.

When I sailed for Europe, in the spring of 1787, it was my intention to return to America the next year, and enjoy in retirement the esteem of my friends, and the repose I was entitled to. I had stood out the storm of one revolution, and had no wish to embark in another. But other scenes and other circumstances than those of contemplated ease were allotted to me. The French revolution was beginning to germinate when I arrived in France. The principles of it were good, they were copied from America, and the men who conducted it were honest. But the fury of faction soon extinguished the one, and sent the other to the scaffold. Of those who began that revolution, I am almost the only survivor, and that through a thousand dangers. I owe this not to the prayers of priests, nor to the piety of hypocrites, but to the continued protection of Providence.

But while I beheld with pleasure the dawn of liberty rising in Europe, I saw with regret the lustre of it fading in America. In less than two years from the time of my departure some distant symptoms painfully suggested the idea that the principles of the revolution were expiring on the soil that produced them. I received at that time a letter from a female literary correspondent, and in my answer to her, I expressed my fears on that head.

I now know from the information I obtain upon the spot, that the impressions that then distressed me, for I was proud of America, were but too well founded. She was turning her back on her own glory, and making hasty strides in the retrograde path of oblivion. But a spark from the altar of *Seventy-six*, unextinguished and unextinguishable through the long night of error, is again lighting up, in every part of the Union, the genuine name of rational liberty.

As the French revolution advanced, it fixed the attention of the world, and drew from the pensioned pen of Edmund Burke a furious attack. This brought me once more on the public theatre of politics, and occasioned the pamphlet *Rights of Man*. It had the greatest run of any work ever published in the English language. The number of copies circulated in England, Scotland, and Ireland, besides translations into foreign languages, was between four and five hundred thousand. The principles of that work were the same as those in *Common Sense*, and the effects would have been the same in England as that had produced in America, could the vote of the nation been quietly taken, or had equal opportunities of consulting or acting existed. The only difference between the two works was, that the one was adapted to the local circumstances of England, and the other to those of America. As to myself, I acted in both cases alike; I relinquished to the people of England, as I had done to those of America, all profits from the work. My reward existed in the ambition to do good, and the independent happiness of my own mind.

But a faction, acting in disguise, was rising in America; they had lost sight of first principles. They were beginning to contemplate government as a profitable monopoly, and the people as hereditary property. It is, therefore, no wonder that the *Rights of Man* was attacked by that faction, and its author continually abused. But let them go on; give them rope enough and they will put an end to their own insignificance. There is too much common sense and independence in America to be long the dupe of any faction, foreign or domestic.

But, in the midst of the freedom we enjoy, the licentiousness of the papers called Federal, (and I know not why they are called so, for they are in their principles anti-federal and despotic,) is a dishonour to the character of the country, and an injury to its reputation and importance abroad. They represent the whole people of America as destitute of public principle and private manners. As to any injury they can do at home to those whom they abuse, or service they can render to those who employ them, it is to be set down to the account of noisy nothingness. It is on themselves the disgrace recoils, for the reflection easily presents itself to every thinking mind, that *those who abuse liberty when they possess it would abuse power could they obtain it*; and, therefore, they may as well take as a general motto, for all such papers, *We and our patrons are not fit to be trusted with power.*

There is in America, more than in any other country, a large body of people who attend quietly to their farms, or follow their several occupations; who pay no regard to the clamours of anonymous scribblers, who think for themselves, and judge of government, not by the fury of newspaper writers, but by the prudent frugality of its measures, and the encouragement it gives to the improvement and prosperity of the country; and who, acting on their own judgment, never come forward in an election but on some important occasion. When this body moves, all the little barkings of scribbling and witless curs pass for nothing. To say to this independent description of men, "You must turn out such and such persons at the next election, for they have taken off a great many taxes, and lessened the expenses of government, they have dismissed my son, or my brother, or myself, from a lucrative office, in which there was nothing to do" — is to show the cloven foot of faction, and preach the language of ill-disguised mortification. In every part of the Union, this faction is in the agonies of death, and in proportion as its fate approaches, gnashes its teeth and struggles. My arrival has struck it as with an hydrophobia, it is like the sight of water to canine madness.

As this letter is intended to announce my arrival to my friends, and to my enemies if I have any, for I ought to have none in America, and as introductory to others that will occasionally follow, I shall close it by detailing the line of conduct I shall pursue.

I have no occasion to ask, and do not intend to accept, any place or office in the government.1 There is none it could give me that would be any ways equal to the profits I could make as an author, for I have an established fame in the literary world, could I reconcile it to my principles to make money by my politics or religion. I must be in every thing what I have ever been, a disinterested volunteer; my proper sphere of action is on the common floor of citizenship, and to honest men I give my hand and my heart freely.

I have some manuscript works to publish, of which I shall give proper notice, and some mechanical affairs to bring forward, that will employ all my leisure time. I shall continue these letters as I see occasion, and as to the low party prints that choose to abuse me, they are welcome; I shall not descend to answer them. I have been too much used to such common stuff to take any notice of it. The government of England honoured me with a thousand martyrdoms, by burning me in effigy in every town in that country, and their hirelings in America may do the same.

Thomas Paine.

City of Washington.

5 | Letters to the Citizens of the United States

II.

from *The National Intelligencer*, November 22, 1802

As the affairs of the country to which I am returned are of more importance to the world, and to me, than of that I have lately left, (for it is through the new world the old must be regenerated, if regenerated at all,) I shall not take up the time of the reader with an account of scenes that have passed in France, many of which are painful to remember and horrid to relate, but come at once to the circumstances in which I find America on my arrival.

Fourteen years, and something more, have produced a change, at least among a part of the people, and I ask myself what it is? I meet or hear of thousands of my former connexions, who are men of the same principles and friendships as when I left them. But a non-descript race, and of equivocal generation, assuming the name of *Federalist*, — a name that describes no character of principle good or bad, and may equally be applied to either, — has since started up with the rapidity of a mushroom, and like a mushroom is withering on its rootless stalk.

Are those men *federalized* to support the liberties of their country or to overturn them? To add to its fair fame or riot on its spoils? The name contains no defined idea. It is like John Adams's definition of a Republic, in his letter to Mr. Wythe of Virginia. *It is,* says he, *an empire of laws and not of men.* But as laws may be bad as well as good, an empire of laws may be the best of all governments or the worst of all tyrannies. But John Adams is a man of paradoxical heresies, and consequently of a bewildered mind. He wrote a book entitled, "A Defence of the American Constitutions," and the principles of it are an attack upon them. But the book is descended to the tomb of forgetfulness, and the best fortune that can attend its author is quietly to follow its fate. John was not born for immortality. But, to return to Federalism.

In the history of parties and the names they assume, it often happens that they finish by the direct contrary principles with which they profess to begin, and thus it has happened with Federalism.

During the time of the old Congress, and prior to the establishment of the federal government, the continental belt was too loosely buckled. The several states were united in name but not in fact, and that nominal union had neither centre nor circle. The laws of one state frequently interferred with, and sometimes opposed, those of another. Commerce between state and state was without protection, and confidence without a point to rest on. The condition the country was then in, was aptly described by Pelatiah Webster, when he said, *"thirteen staves and ne'er a hoop will not make a barrel."*

If, then, by *Federalist* is to be understood one who was for cementing the Union by a general government operating equally over all the States, in all matters that embraced the common interest, and to which the authority of the States severally was not adequate, for no one State can make laws to bind another; if, I say, by a *Federalist* is meant a person of this description, (and this is the origin of the name,) *I ought to stand first on the list of Federalists*, for the proposition for establishing a general government over the Union, came originally from me in 1783, in a written Memorial to

7 | Letters to the Citizens of the United States

Chancellor Livingston, then Secretary for Foreign Affairs to Congress, Robert Morris, Minister of Finance, and his associate, Gouverneur Morris, all of whom are now living; and we had a dinner and conference at Robert Morris's on the subject. The occasion was as follows:

Congress had proposed a duty of five per cent. on imported articles, the money to be applied as a fund towards paying the interest of loans to be borrowed in Holland. The resolve was sent to the several States to be enacted into a law. Rhode Island absolutely refused. I was at the trouble of a journey to Rhode Island to reason with them on the subject. Some other of the States enacted it with alterations, each one as it pleased. Virginia adopted it, and afterwards repealed it, and the affair came to nothing.

It was then visible, at least to me, that either Congress must frame the laws necessary for the Union, and send them to the several States to be enregistered without any alteration, which would in itself appear like usurpation on one part and passive obedience on the other, or some method must be devised to accomplish the same end by constitutional principles; and the proposition I made in the memorial was, *to add a continental legislature to Congress, to be elected by the several States*. The proposition met the full approbation of the gentlemen to whom it was addressed, and the conversation turned on the manner of bringing it forward. Gouverneur Morris, in walking with me after dinner, wished me to throw out the idea in the newspaper; I replied, that I did not like to be always the proposer of new things, that it would have too assuming an appearance; and besides, that *I did not think the country was quite wrong enough to be put right*.

I remember giving the same reason to Dr. Rush, at Philadelphia, and to General Gates, at whose quarters I spent a day on my return from Rhode Island; and I suppose they will remember it, because the observation seemed to strike them.

But the embarrassments increasing, as they necessarily must from the want of a better cemented union, the State of Virginia proposed holding a commercial convention, and that convention, which was not sufficiently numerous, proposed that another convention, with more extensive and better defined powers, should be held at Philadelphia, May 10, 1787.

When the plan of the Federal Government, formed by this Convention, was proposed and submitted to the consideration of the several States, it was strongly objected to in each of them. But the objections were not on anti-federal grounds, but on constitutional points. Many were shocked at the idea of placing what is called Executive Power in the hands of a single individual. To them it had too much the form and appearance of a military government, or a despotic one. Others objected that the powers given to a president were too great, and that in the hands of an ambitious and designing man it might grow into tyranny, as it did in England under Oliver Cromwell, and as it has since done in France. A Republic must not only be so in its principles, but in its forms. The Executive part of the Federal government was made for a man, and those who consented, against their judgment, to place Executive Power in the hands of a single individual, reposed more on the supposed moderation of the person they had in view, than on the wisdom of the measure itself.

Two considerations, however, overcame all objections. The one was, the absolute necessity of a Federal Government. The other, the rational reflection, that as government in America is founded on the representative system any error in the first essay could be reformed by the same quiet and rational process by which the Constitution was formed, and that either by the generation then living, or by those who were to succeed.

9 | Letters to the Citizens of the United States

If ever America lose sight of this principle, she will no longer be the *land of liberty*. The father will become the assassin of the rights of the son, and his descendants be a race of slaves.

As many thousands who were minors are grown up to manhood since the name of *Federalist* began, it became necessary, for their information, to go back and show the origin of the name, which is now no longer what it originally was; but it was the more necessary to do this, in order to bring forward, in the open face of day, the apostacy of those who first called themselves Federalists.

To them it served as a cloak for treason, a mask for tyranny. Scarcely were they placed in the seat of power and office, than Federalism was to be destroyed, and the representative system of government, the pride and glory of America, and the palladium of her liberties, was to be overthrown and abolished. The next generation was not to be free. The son was to bend his neck beneath the father's foot, and live, deprived of his rights, under hereditary control.

Among the men of this apostate description, is to be ranked the ex-president *John Adams*. It has been the political career of this man to begin with hypocrisy, proceed with arrogance, and finish in contempt. May such be the fate of all such characters.

I have had doubts of John Adams ever since the year 1776. In a conversation with me at that time, concerning the pamphlet *Common Sense*, he censured it because it attacked the English form of government. John was for independence because he expected to be made great by it; but it was not difficult to perceive, for the surliness of his temper makes him an awkward hypocrite, that his head was as full of kings, queens, and knaves, as a pack of cards. But John has lost deal.

When a man has a concealed project in his brain that he wants to bring forward, and fears will not succeed, he begins with it as physicians do by suspected poison, try it first on an animal; if it agree with the stomach of the animal, he makes further experiments, and this was the way John took. His brain was teeming with projects to overturn the liberties of America, and the representative system of government, and he began by hinting it in little companies.

The secretary of John Jay, an excellent painter and a poor politician, told me, in presence of another American, Daniel Parker, that in a company where himself was present, John Adams talked of making the government hereditary, and that as Mr. Washington had no children, it should be made hereditary in the family of Lund Washington.

John had not impudence enough to propose himself in the first instance, as the old French Normandy baron did, who offered to come over to be king of America, and if Congress did not accept his offer, that they would give him thirty thousand pounds for the generosity of it but John, like a mole, was grubbing his way to it under ground. He knew that Lund Washington was unknown, for nobody had heard of him, and that as the president had no children to succeed him, the vice-president had, and if the treason had succeeded, and the hint with it, the goldsmith might be sent for to take measure of the head of John or of his son for a golden wig.

In this case, the good people of Boston might have for a king the man they have rejected as a delegate. The representative system is fatal to ambition.

Knowing, as I do, the consummate vanity of John Adams, and the shallowness of his judgment, I can easily picture to myself that when he arrived at the Federal City he was strutting in the pomp of his imagination before the presidential house, or in the audience hall, and exulting in the language of Nebuchadnezzar, "Is not this great Babylon, that I have built for the honour of my Majesty!" But

11 | Letters to the Citizens of the United States

in that unfortunate hour, or soon after, John, like Nebuchadnezzar, was driven from among men, and fled with the speed of a post-horse.

Some of John Adams's loyal subjects, I see, have been to present him with an address on his birthday; but the language they use is too tame for the occasion. Birthday addresses, like birthday odes, should not creep along like mildrops down a cabbage leaf, but roll in a torrent of poetical metaphor. I will give them a specimen for the next year. Here it is —

When an Ant, in travelling over the globe, lift up its foot, and put it again on the ground, it shakes the earth to its centre: but when YOU, the mighty Ant of the East, was born, &c. &c. &c., the centre jumped upon the surface.

This, gentlemen, is the proper style of addresses from *well-bred* ants to the monarch of the ant hills; and as I never take pay for preaching, praying, politics, or poetry, I make you a present of it. Some people talk of impeaching John Adams; but I am for softer measures. I would keep him to make fun of. He will then answer one of the ends for which he was born, and he ought to be thankful that I am arrived to take his part. I voted in earnest to save the life of one unfortunate king, and I now vote in jest to save another. It is my fate to be always plagued with fools. But to return to Federalism and apostacy.

The plan of the leaders of the faction was to overthrow the liberties of the new world, and place government on the corrupt system of the old. They wanted to hold their power by a more lasting tenure than the choice of their constituents. It is impossible to account for their conduct and the measures they adopted on any other ground.

But to accomplish that object, a standing army and a prodigal revenue must be raised; and to obtain these, pretences must be invented to deceive. Alarms of dangers that did not exist even in imagination, but in the direct spirit of lying, were spread abroad. Apostacy stalked through the land in the garb of patriotism, and the torch of treason blinded for a while the flame of liberty.

For what purpose could an army of twenty-five thousand men be wanted? A single reflection might have taught the most credulous that while the war raged between France and England, neither could spare a man to invade America. For what purpose, then, could it be wanted? The case carries its own explanation. It was wanted for the purpose of destroying the representative system, for it could be employed for no other. Are these men Federalists? If they are, they are federalized to deceive and to destroy.

The rage against Dr. Logan's patriotic and voluntary mission to France was excited by the shame they felt at the detection of the false alarms they had circulated. As to the opposition given by the remnant of the faction to the repeal of the taxes laid on during the former administration, it is easily accounted for. The repeal of those taxes was a sentence of condemnation on those who laid them on, and in the opposition they gave in that repeal, they are to be considered in the light of criminals standing on their defence, and the country has passed judgment upon them.

Thomas Paine.

City of Washington, Lovett's Hotel, Nov. 19, 1802.

III.

from *The National Intelligencer*, November 29, 1802

To elect, and to reject, is the prerogative of a free people.

Since the establishment of Independence, no period has arrived that so decidedly proves the excellence of the representative system of government, and its superiority over every other, as the time we now live in. Had America been cursed with John Adams's *hereditary Monarchy*, or Alexander Hamilton's *Senate for life*, she must have sought, in the doubtful contest of civil war, what she now obtains by the expression of public will. An appeal to elections decides better than an appeal to the sword.

The Reign of Terror that raged in America during the latter end of the Washington administration, and the whole of that of Adams, is enveloped in mystery to me. That there were men in the government hostile to the representative system, was once their boast, though it is now their overthrow, and therefore the fact is established against them. But that so large a mass of the people should become the dupes of those who were loading them with taxes in order to load them with chains, and deprive them of the right of election, can be ascribed only to that species of wildfire rage, lighted up by falsehood, that not only acts without reflection, but is too impetuous to make any.

There is a general and striking difference between the genuine effects of truth itself, and the effects of falsehood believed to be truth. Truth is naturally benign; but false-hood believed to be truth is always furious. The former delights in serenity, is mild and persuasive, and seeks not the auxiliary aid of invention. The latter sticks at nothing. It has naturally no morals. Every lie is welcome that suits its purpose. It is the innate character of the thing to act in this manner, and the criterion by which it may be known, whether in politics or religion. When any thing is attempted to be supported by lying, it is presumptive evidence that the thing so supported is a lie also. The stock on which a lie can be grafted must be of the same species as the graft.

What is become of the mighty clamour of French invasion, and the cry that our country is in danger, and taxes and armies must be raised to defend it? The danger is fled with the faction that created it, and what is worst of all, the money is fled too. It is I only that have committed the hostility of invasion, and all the artillery of popguns are prepared for action. Poor fellows, how they foam! They set half their own partisans in laughter; for among ridiculous things nothing is more ridiculous than ridiculous rage. But I hope they will not leave off. I shall lose half my greatness when they cease to lie.

So far as respects myself, I have reason to believe, and a right to say, that the leaders of the Reign of Terror in America and the leaders of the Reign of Terror in France, during the time of Robespierre, were in character the same sort of men; or how is it to be accounted for, that I was persecuted by both at the same time? When I was voted out of the French Convention, the reason assigned for it was, that I was a foreigner. When Robespierre had me seized in the night, and imprisoned in the Luxembourg, (where I remained eleven months,) he assigned no reason for it. But when he proposed bringing me to the tribunal, which was like sending me at

15 | Letters to the Citizens of the United States

once to the scaffold, he then assigned a reason, and the reason was, *for the interests of America as well as of* France. *"Pour les interêts de l' Amérique autant que de la France."* The words are in his own handwriting, and reported to the Convention by the committee appointed to examine his papers, and are printed in their report, with this reflection added to them, "Why Thomas Paine more than another? Because he contributed to the liberty of both worlds."

There must have been a coalition in sentiment, if not in fact, between the Terrorists of America and the Terrorists of France, and Robespierre must have known it, or he could not have had the idea of putting America into the bill of accusation against me. Yet these men, these Terrorists of the new world, who were waiting in the devotion of their hearts for the joyful news of my destruction, are the same banditti who are now bellowing in all the hacknied language of hacknied hypocrisy, about humanity, and piety, and often about something they call infidelity, and they finish with the chorus of *Crucify him, crucify him*. I am become so famous among them, they cannot eat or drink without me. I serve them as a standing dish, and they cannot make up a bill of fare if I am not in it.

But there is one dish, and that the choicest of all, that they have not presented on the table, and it is time they should. They have not yet *accused Providence of Infidelity*. Yet according to their outrageous piety, she must be as bad as Thomas Paine; she has protected him in all his dangers, patronized him in all his undertakings, encouraged him in all his ways, and rewarded him at last by bringing him in safety and in health to the Promised Land. This is more than she did by the Jews, the chosen people, that they tell us she brought out of the land of Egypt, and out of the house of bondage; for they all died in the wilderness, and Moses too.

I was one of the nine members that composed the first Committee of Constitution. Six of them have been destroyed. Sièyes and myself have survived — he by bending with the times, and I by not bending. The other survivor joined Robespierre, he was seized and imprisoned in his turn, and sentenced to transportation. He has since apologized to me for having signed the warrant, by saying he felt himself in danger and was obliged to do it.

Herault Sechelles, an acquaintance of Mr. Jefferson, and a good patriot, was my *suppléant* as member of the Committee of Constitution, that is, he was to supply my place, if I had not accepted or had resigned, being next in number of votes to me. He was imprisoned in the Luxembourg with me, was taken to the tribunal and the guillotine, and I, his principal, was left.

There were two foreigners in the Convention, Anarcharsis Clootz and myself. We were both put out of the Convention by the same vote, arrested by the same order, and carried to prison together the same night. He was taken to the guillotine, and I was again left. Joel Barlow was with us when we went to prison.

Joseph Lebon, one of the vilest characters that ever existed, and who made the streets of Arras run with blood, was my *suppléant*, as member of the Convention for the department of the Pas de Calais. When I was put out of the Convention he came and took my place. When I was liberated from prison and voted again into the Convention, he was sent to the same prison and took my place there, and he was sent to the guillotine instead of me. He supplied my place all the way through.

One hundred and sixty-eight persons were taken out of the Luxembourg in one night, and a hundred and sixty of them guillotined next day, of which I now know I was to have been one; and the manner I escaped that fate is curious, and has all the appearance of accident.

The room in which I was lodged was on the ground floor, and one

17 | Letters to the Citizens of the United States

of a long range of rooms under a gallery, and the door of it opened outward and flat against the wall; so that when it was open the inside of the door appeared outward, and the contrary when it was shut. I had three comrades, fellow prisoners with me, Joseph Vanhuele, of Bruges, since President of the Municipality of that town, Michael Rubyns, and Charles Bastini of Louvain.

When persons by scores and by hundreds were to be taken out of the prison for the guillotine it was always done in the night, and those who performed that office had a private mark or signal, by which they knew what rooms to go to, and what number to take. We, as I have stated, were four, and the door of our room was marked, unobserved by us, with that number in chalk; but it happened, if happening is a proper word, that the mark was put on when the door was open, and flat against the wall, and thereby came on the inside when we shut it at night, and the destroying angel passed by it. A few days after this, Robespierre fell, and Mr. Monroe arrived and reclaimed me, and invited me to his house.

During the whole of my imprisonment, prior to the fall of Robespierre, there was no time when I could think my life worth twenty-four hours, and my mind was made up to meet its fate. The Americans in Paris went in a body to the Convention to reclaim me, but without success. There was no party among them with respect to me.

My only hope then rested on the government of America, that it would *remember me*. But the icy heart of ingratitude, in whatever man it be placed, has neither feeling nor sense of honour. The letter of Mr. Jefferson has served to wipe away the reproach, and done justice to the mass of the people of America.

When a party was forming, in the latter end of 1777, and beginning of 1778, of which John Adams was one, to remove Mr. Washington from the command of the army on the complaint that *he did nothing,* I wrote the fifth number of the *Crisis,* and published it at Lancaster, (Congress then being at Yorktown, in Pennsylvania), to ward off that meditated blow; for though I well knew that the black times of '76 were the natural consequence of his want of military judgment in the choice of positions into which the army was put about New York and New Jersey, I could see no possible advantage, and nothing but mischief, that could arise by distracting the army into parties, which would have been the case had the intended motion gone on.

General [Charles] Lee, who with a sarcastic genius joined a great fund of military knowledge, was perfectly right when he said *"We have no business on islands, and in the bottom of bogs, where the enemy, by the aid of its ships, can bring its whole force against a part of ours and shut it up."* This had like to have been the case at New York, and it was the case at Fort Washington, and would have been the case at Fort Lee if General [Nathaniel] Greene had not moved instantly off on the first news of the enemy's approach. I was with Greene through the whole of that affair, and know it perfectly.

But though I came forward in defence of Mr. Washington when he was attacked, and made the best that could be made of a series of blunders that had nearly ruined the country, he left me to perish when I was in prison. But as I told him of it in his life-time, I should not now bring it up if the ignorant impertinence of some of the Federal papers, who are pushing Mr. Washington forward as their stalking horse, did not make it necessary.

That gentleman did not perform his part in the Revolution better, nor with more honour, than I did mine, and the one part was as necessary as the other. He accepted as a present, (though he was already rich,) a hundred thousand acres of land in America, and left me to occupy six foot of earth in France. I wish, for his own reputation, he had acted with more justice. But it was always

19 | Letters to the Citizens of the United States

known of Mr. Washington, by those who best knew him, that he was of such an icy and death-like constitution, that he neither loved his friends nor hated his enemies. But, be this as it may, I see no reason that a difference between Mr. Washington and me should be made a theme of discord with other people. There are those who may see merit in both, without making themselves partisans of either, and with this reflection I close the subject.

As to the hypocritical abuse thrown out by the Federalists on other subjects, I recommend to them the observance of a commandment that existed before either Christian or Jew existed:

* Thou shalt make a covenant with thy senses:
* With thine eye, that it behold no evil,
* With thine ear, that it hear no evil,
* With thy tongue, that it speak no evil,
* With thy hands, that they commit no evil.

If the Federalists will follow this commandment, they will leave off lying.

Thomas Paine.

Federal City, Lovett's Hotel, Nov. 26, 1802.

20 | Letters to the Citizens of the United States

IV.

from The National Intelligencer, December 6, 1802

As Congress is on the point of meeting, the public papers will necessarily be occupied with the debates of the ensuing session, and as, in consequence of my long absence from America, my private affairs require my attendance, (for it is necessary I do this, or I could not preserve, as I do, my independence,) I shall close my address to the public with this letter.

I congratulate them on the success of the late elections, and *that* with the additional confidence, that while honest men are chosen and wise measures pursued, neither the treason of apostacy, masked under the name of Federalism, of which I have spoken in my second letter, nor the intrigues of foreign emissaries, acting in concert with that mask, can prevail.

As to the licentiousness of the papers calling themselves *Federal*, a name that apostacy has taken, it can hurt nobody but the party or the persons who support such papers. There is naturally a wholesome pride in the public mind that revolts at open vulgarity. It feels itself dishonoured even by hearing it, as a chaste woman feels dishonour by hearing obscenity she cannot avoid. It can smile at wit, or be diverted with strokes of satirical humour, but it detests the *blackguard*.

The same sense of propriety that governs in private companies, governs in public life. If a man in company runs his wit upon another, it may draw a smile from some persons present, but as soon as he turns a blackguard in his language the company gives him up; and it is the same in public life. The event of the late election shows this to be true; for in proportion as those papers have become more and more vulgar and abusive, the elections have gone more and more against the party they support, or that supports them. Their predecessor, *Porcupine* [William Cobbett] had wit — these scribblers have none. But as soon as his *blackguardism* (for it is the proper name of it) outran his wit, he was abandoned by every body but the English Minister who protected him.

The Spanish proverb says, *"there never was a cover large enough to hide itself"*; and the proverb applies to the case of those papers and the shattered remnant of the faction that supports them. The falsehoods they fabricate, and the abuse they circulate, is a cover to hide something from being seen, but it is not large enough to hide itself. It is as a tub thrown out to the whale to prevent its attacking and sinking the vessel. They want to draw the attention of the public from thinking about, or inquiring into, the measures of the late administration, and the reason why so much public money was raised and expended; and so far as a lie today, and a new one tomorrow, will answer this purpose, it answers theirs. It is nothing to them whether they be believed or not, for if the negative purpose be answered the main point is answered, to them.

He that picks your pocket always tries to make you look another way. "Look," says he, "at yon man t'other side the street — what a nose he has got? — Lord, yonder is a chimney on fire! — Do you see yon man going along in the salamander great coat? That is the very man that stole one of Jupiter's satellites, and sold it to a countryman for a gold watch, and it set his breeches on fire!" Now the man that has his hand in your pocket, does not care a farthing whether you believe what he says or not. All his aim is to prevent your looking at him; and this is the case with the remnant of the Federal faction. The leaders of it have imposed upon the country, and they want to turn the attention of it from the subject.

In taking up any public matter, I have never made it a consideration, and never will, whether it be popular or unpopular; but whether it be *right* or *wrong*. The right will always become the popular, if it has courage to show itself, and the shortest way is always a straight line.

I despise expedients, they are the gutter-hole of politics, and the sink where reputation dies. In the present case, as in every other, I cannot be accused of using any; and I have no doubt but thousands will hereafter be ready to say, as Gouverneur Morris said to me, after having abused me pretty handsomely in Congress for the opposition I gave the fraudulent demand of Silas Deane of two thousand pounds sterling: *"Well, we were all duped, and I among the rest!"*

Were the late administration to be called upon to give reasons for the expence it put the country to, it can give none. The danger of an invasion was a bubble that served as a cover to raise taxes and armies to be employed on some other purpose. But if the people of America believed it true, the cheerfulness with which they supported those measures and paid those taxes is an evidence of their patriotism; and if they supposed me their enemy, though in that supposition they did me injustice, it was not injustice in them. He that acts as he believes, though he may act wrong, is not conscious of wrong.

But though there was no danger, no thanks are due to the late administration for it. They sought to blow up a flame between the two countries; and so intent were they upon this, that they went out of their way to accomplish it. In a letter which the Secretary of

State, Timothy Pickering, wrote to Mr. Skipwith, the American Consul at Paris, he broke off from the official subject of his letter, to *thank God* in very exulting language, *that the Russians had cut the French army to pieces.* Mr. Skipwith, after showing me the letter, very prudently concealed it.

It was the injudicious and wicked acrimony of this letter, and some other like conduct of the then Secretary of State, that occasioned me, in a letter to a friend in the government, to say, that if there was any official business to be done in France, till a regular Minister could be appointed, it could not be trusted to a more proper person than Mr. Skipwith. *"He is,"* said I, *"an honest man, and will do business, and that with good manners to the government he is commissioned to act with. A faculty which that bear, Timothy Pickering, wanted, and which the bear of that bear, John Adams, never possessed."*

In another letter to the same friend, in 1797, and which was put unsealed under cover to Colonel Burr, I expressed a satisfaction that Mr. Jefferson, since he was not president, had accepted the vice presidency; *"for,"* said I, *"John Adams has such a talent for blundering and offending, it will be necessary to keep an eye over him."* He has now sufficiently proved, that though I have not the spirit of prophecy, I have the gift of *judging right.*

And all the world knows, for it cannot help knowing, that to judge *rightly* and to write *clearly,* and that upon all sorts of subjects, to be able to command thought and as it were to play with it at pleasure, and be always master of one's temper in writing, is the faculty only of a serene mind, and the attribute of a happy and philosophical temperament.

The scribblers, who know me not, and who fill their papers with paragraphs about me, besides their want of talents, drink too many slings and drams in a morning to have any chance with me. But,

25 | Letters to the Citizens of the United States

poor fellows, they must do something for the little pittance they get from their employers. This is my apology for them.

My anxiety to get back to America was great for many years. It is the country of my heart, and the place of my political and literary birth. It was the American revolution that made me an author, and forced into action the mind that had been dormant, and had no wish for public life, nor has it now. By the accounts I received, she appeared to me to be going wrong, and that some meditated treason against her liberties lurked at the bottom of her government. I heard that my friends were oppressed, and I longed to take my stand among them, and if other times *to try men's souls* were to arrive, that I might bear my share. But my efforts to return were ineffectual.

As soon as Mr. Monroe had made a good standing with the French government, for the conduct of his predecessor [Morris] had made his reception as Minister difficult, he wanted to send despatches to his own government by a person to whom he could confide a verbal communication, and he fixed his choice on me. He then applied to the Committee of Public Safety for a passport; but as I had been voted again into the Convention, it was only the Convention that could give the passport; and as an application to them for that purpose, would have made my going publicly known, I was obliged to sustain the disappointment, and Mr. Monroe to lose the opportunity.

When that gentleman left France to return to America, I was to have gone with him. It was fortunate I did not. The vessel he sailed in was visited by a British frigate, that searched every part of it, and down to the hold, for Thomas Paine. I then went, the same year, to embark at Havre. But several British frigates were cruizing in sight of the port who knew I was there, and I had to return again to Paris.

Seeing myself thus cut off from every opportunity that was in my power to command, I wrote to Mr. Jefferson, that, if the fate of the election should put him in the chair of the presidency, and he should have occasion to send a frigate to France, he would give me the opportunity of returning by it, which he did. But I declined coming by the *Maryland*, the vessel that was offered me, and waited for the frigate that was to bring the new Minister, Mr. Chancellor Livingston, to France. But that frigate was ordered round to the Mediterranean; and as at that time the war was over, and the British cruisers called in, I could come any way. I then agreed to come with Commodore Barney in a vessel he had engaged. It was again fortunate I did not, for the vessel sank at sea, and the people were preserved in the boat.

Had half the number of evils befallen me that the number of dangers amount to through which I have been preserved, there are those who would ascribe it to the wrath of heaven; why then do they not ascribe my preservation to the protecting favour of heaven? Even in my worldly concerns I have been blessed. The little property I left in America, and which I cared nothing about, not even to receive the rent of it, has been increasing in the value of its capital more than eight hundred dollars every year, for the fourteen years and more that I have been absent from it. I am now in my circumstances independent; and my economy makes me rich. As to my health, it is perfectly good, and I leave the world to judge of the stature of my mind. I am in every instance a living contradiction to the mortified Federalists.

In my publications, I follow the rule I began with in *Common Sense*, that is, to consult nobody, nor to let any body see what I write till it appears publicly. Were I to do otherwise, the case would be, that between the timidity of some, who are so afraid of doing wrong that they never do right, the puny judgment of others, and the

27 | Letters to the Citizens of the United States

despicable craft of preferring *expedient to right*, as if the world was a world of babies in leading strings, I should get forward with nothing.

My path is a right line, as straight and clear to me as a ray of light. The boldness (if they will have it to be so) with which I speak on any subject, is a compliment to the judgment of the reader. It is like saying to him, *I treat you as a man and not as a child*. With respect to any worldly object, as it is impossible to discover any in me, therefore what I do, and my manner of doing it, ought to be ascribed to a good motive.

In a great affair, where the happiness of man is at stake, I love to work for nothing; and so fully am I under the influence of this principle, that I should lose the spirit, the pleasure, and the pride of it, were I conscious that I looked for reward; and with this declaration, I take my leave for the present.

Thomas Paine.

Federal City, Lovett's Hotel, Dec. 3, 1802.

V.

from *The National Intelligencer*, February 2, 1802

It is always the interest of a far greater part of the nation to have a thing right than to have it wrong; and therefore, in a country whose government is founded on the system of election and representation, the fate of every party is decided by its principles.

As this system is the only form and principle of government by which liberty can be preserved, and the only one that can embrace all the varieties of a great extent of country, it necessarily follows, that to have the representation real, the election must be real; and that where the election is a fiction, the representation is a fiction also. *Like will always produce like.*

A great deal has been said and written concerning the conduct of Mr. Burr, during the late contest, in the federal legislature, whether Mr. Jefferson or Mr. Burr should be declared President of the United States. Mr. Burr has been accused of intriguing to obtain the Presidency. Whether this charge be substantiated or not makes little or no part of the purport of this letter. There is a point of much higher importance to attend to than any thing that relates to the individual Mr. Burr: For the great point is not whether Mr. Burr has intrigued, but whether the legislature has intrigued with *him*.

Mr. Ogden, a relation of one of the senators of New Jersey of the same name, and of the party assuming the style of Federalists, has written a letter published in the New York papers, signed with his name, the purport of which is to exculpate Mr. Burr from the charges brought against him. In this letter he says:

"When about to return from Washington, two or three *members of Congress* of the federal party spoke to me of *their views*, as to the election of a president, desiring me to converse with Colonel Burr on the subject, and to ascertain *whether he would enter into terms*. On my return to New York I called on Colonel Burr, and communicated the above to him. He explicitly declined the explanation, and did neither propose nor agree to any terms."

How nearly is human cunning allied to folly! The animals to whom nature has given the faculty we call *cunning*, know always when to use it, and use it wisely; but when man descends to cunning, he blunders and betrays.

Mr. Ogden's letter is intended to exculpate Mr. Burr from the charge of intriguing to obtain the presidency; and the letter that he (Ogden) writes for this purpose is direct evidence against his party in Congress, that they intrigued with Burr to obtain him for President, and employed him (Ogden) for the purpose. To save *Aaron*, he betrays *Moses*, and then turns informer against the *Golden Calf*.

It is but of little importance to the world to know if Mr. Burr listened to an intriguing proposal, but it is of great importance to the constituents to know if their representatives in Congress made one. The ear can commit no crime, but the tongue may; and therefore the right policy is to drop Mr. Burr, as being only the hearer, and direct the whole charge against the Federal faction in Congress as the active original culprit, or, if the priests will have scripture for it, as the serpent that beguiled Eve.

The plot of the intrigue was to make Mr. Burr President, on the private condition of his agreeing to, and entering into, terms with them, that is, with the proposers. Had then the election been made, the country, knowing nothing of this private and illegal transaction, would have supposed, for who could have supposed otherwise, that it had a President according to the forms, principles, and intention of the constitution. No such thing. Every form, principle, and intention of the constitution would have been violated; and instead of a President, it would have had a mute, a sort of image, hand-bound and tongue-tied, the dupe and slave of a party, placed on the theatre of the United States, and acting the farce of President.

It is of little importance, in a constitutional sense, to know what the terms to be proposed might be, because any terms other than those which the constitution prescribes to a President are criminal. Neither do I see how Mr. Burr, or any other person put in the same condition, could have taken the oath prescribed by the constitution to a President, which is, *"I do solemnly swear* (or affirm,) *that I will faithfully execute the office of President of the United States, and will to the best of my ability preserve, protect, and defend the Constitution of the United States."*

How, I ask, could such a person have taken such an oath, knowing at the same time that he had entered into the Presidency on terms unknown in the Constitution, and private, and which would deprive him of the freedom and power of acting as President of the United States, agreeably to his constitutional oath?

Mr. Burr, by not agreeing to terms, has escaped the danger to which they exposed him, and the perjury that would have followed, and also the punishment annexed thereto. Had he accepted the Presidency on terms unknown in the constitution, and private, and had the transaction afterwards transpired, (which it most probably would, for roguery is a thing difficult to conceal,) it would have produced a sensation in the country too violent to be quieted, and too just to be resisted; and in any case the election must have been void.

But what are we to think of those members of Congress, who having taken an oath of the same constitutional import as the oath of the President, violate that oath by tampering to obtain a President on private conditions. If this is not sedition against the constitution and the country, it is difficult to define what sedition in a representative can be.

Say not that this statement of the case is the effect of personal or party resentment. No. It is the effect of *sincere concern* that such corruption, of which this is but a sample, should, in the space of a few years, have crept into a country that had the fairest opportunity that Providence ever gave, within the knowledge of history, of making itself an illustrious example to the world.

What the terms were, or were to be, it is probable we never shall know; or what is more probable, that feigned ones, if any, will be given. But from the conduct of the party since that time we may conclude, that no taxes would have been taken off, that the clamour for war would have been kept up, new expences incurred, and taxes and offices increased in consequence; and, among the articles of a private nature, that the leaders in this seditious traffic were to stipulate with the mock President for lucrative appointments for themselves.

But if these plotters against the Constitution understood their business, and they had been plotting long enough to be masters of it, a single article would have comprehended every thing, which is, *That the President (thus made) should be governed in all cases whatsoever by a private junto appointed by themselves.* They could then, through the medium of a mock President, have negatived all bills which their party in Congress could not have opposed with success, and reduced representation to a nullity.

33 | Letters to the Citizens of the United States

The country has been imposed upon, and the real culprits are but few; and as it is necessary for the peace, harmony, and honour of the Union, to separate the deceiver from the deceived, the betrayer from the betrayed, that men who once were friends, and that in the worst of times, should be friends again, it is necessary, as a beginning, that this dark business be brought to full investigation. Ogden's letter is direct evidence of the fact of tampering to obtain a conditional President. He knows the two or three members of Congress that commissioned him, and they know who commissioned them.

Thomas Paine.

Federal City, Lovett's Hotel, January 29, 1803.

VI.

from the Philadelphia Aurora, May 14, 1803

Religion and War is the cry of the Federalists; Morality and Peace the voice of Republicans. The union of Morality and Peace is congenial; but that of Religion and War is a paradox, and the solution of it is hypocrisy.

The leaders of the Federalists have no judgment; their plans no consistency of parts; and want of consistency is the natural consequence of want of principle.

They exhibit to the world the curious spectacle of an *Opposition* without a *cause*, and conduct without system. Were they, as doctors, to prescribe medicine as they practise politics, they would poison their patients with destructive compounds.

There are not two things more opposed to each other than War and Religion; and yet, in the double game those leaders have to play, the one is necessarily the theme of their politics, and the other the text of their sermons. The week-day orator of Mars, and the Sunday preacher of Federal Grace, play like gamblers into each other's hands, and this they call Religion.

Though hypocrisy can counterfeit every virtue, and become the associate of every vice, it requires a great dexterity of craft to give it the power of deceiving. A painted sun may glisten, but it cannot warm. For hypocrisy to personate virtue successfully it must know and feel what virtue is, and as it cannot long do this, it cannot long deceive. When an orator foaming for War breathes forth in another sentence a *plaintive piety of words*, he may as well write "hypocrisy" on his front.

The late attempt of the Federal leaders in Congress (for they acted without the knowledge of their constituents) to plunge the country into War, merits not only reproach but indignation. It was madness, conceived in ignorance and acted in wickedness. The head and the heart went partners in the crime.

A neglect of punctuality in the performance of a treaty is made a *cause* of war by the *Barbary powers*, and of remonstrance and explanation by *civilized Powers*. The Mahometans of Barbary negociate by the sword — they seize first, and expostulate afterwards; and the federal leaders have been labouring to *barbarize* the United States by adopting the practice of the Barbary States, and this they call honour. Let their honour and their hypocrisy go weep together, for both are defeated. Their present Administration is too moral for hypocrites, and too economical for public spendthrifts.

A man the least acquainted with diplomatic affairs must know that a neglect in punctuality is not one of the legal causes of war, unless that neglect be confirmed by a refusal to perform; and even then it depends upon circumstances connected with it. The world would be in continual quarrels and war, and commerce be annihilated, if Algerine policy was the law of nations.

And were America, instead of becoming an example to the old world of good and moral government and civil manners, or, if they like it better, of gentlemanly conduct towards other nations, to set up the character of ruffian, that of *word and blow, and the blow first*, and thereby give the example of pulling down the little that civilization has gained upon barbarism, her Independence, instead

37 | Letters to the Citizens of the United States

of being an honour and a blessing, would become a curse upon the world and upon herself.

The conduct of the Barbary powers, though unjust in principle, is suited to their prejudices, situation, and circumstances. The crusades of the church to exterminate them fixed in their minds the unobliterated belief that every Christian power was their mortal enemy. Their religious prejudices, therefore, suggest the policy, which their situation and circumstances protect them in. As a people, they are neither commercial nor agricultural, they neither import nor export, have no property floating on the seas, nor ships and cargoes in the ports of foreign nations. No retaliation, therefore, can be acted upon them, and they sin secure from punishment.

But this is not the case with the United States. If she sins as a Barbary power, she must answer for it as a Civilized one. Her commerce is continually passing on the seas exposed to capture, and her ships and cargoes in foreign ports to detention and reprisal. An act of War committed by her in the Mississippi would produce a War against the commerce of the Atlantic States, and the latter would have to curse the policy that provoked the former. In every point, therefore, in which the character and interest of the United States be considered, it would ill become her to set an example contrary to the policy and custom of Civilized powers, and practised only by the Barbary powers, that of striking before she expostulates.

But can any man, calling himself a Legislator, and supposed by his constituents to know something of his duty, be so ignorant as to imagine that seizing on New Orleans would finish the affair or even contribute towards it? On the contrary it would have made it worse.

The treaty right of deposite at New Orleans, and the right of the navigation of the Mississippi into the Gulph of Mexico, are distant things. New Orleans is more than an hundred miles in the country from the mouth of the river, and, as a place of deposite, is of no value if the mouth of the river be shut, which either France or Spain could do, and which our possession of New Orleans could neither prevent or remove.

New Orleans in our possession, by an act of hostility, would have become a blockaded port, and consequently of no value to the western people as a place of deposite. Since, therefore, an interruption had arisen to the commerce of the western states, and until the matter could be brought to a fair explanation, it was of less injury to have the port shut and the river open, than to have the river shut and the port in our possession.

That New Orleans could be taken required no stretch of policy to plan, nor spirit of enterprize to effect. It was like marching behind a man to knock him down: and the dastardly slyness of such an attack would have stained the fame of the United States. Where there is no danger cowards are bold, and Captain Bobadils are to be found in the Senate as well as on the stage. Even *Gouverneur*, on such a march, dare have shown a leg.

The people of the western country to whom the Mississippi serves as an inland sea to their commerce, must be supposed to understand the circumstances of that commerce better than a man who is a stranger to it; and as they have shown no approbation of the war-whoop measures of the Federal senators, it becomes presumptive evidence they disapprove them. This is a new mortification for those war-whoop politicians; for the case is, that finding themselves losing ground and withering away in the Atlantic States, they laid hold of the affair of New Orleans in the vain hope of rooting and reinforcing themselves in the western States; and they did this without perceiving that it was one of those ill judged hypocritical expedients in politics, that whether it succeeded or failed the event would be the same.

Had their motion [that of Ross and Morris] succeeded, it would have endangered the commerce of the Atlantic States and ruined their reputation there; and on the other hand the attempt to make a tool of the western people was so badly concealed as to extinguish all credit with them.

But hypocrisy is a vice of sanguine constitution. It flatters and promises itself every thing; and it has yet to learn, with respect to moral and political reputation, it is less dangerous to offend than to deceive.

To the measures of administration, supported by the firmness and integrity of the majority in Congress, the United States owe, as far as human means are concerned, the preservation of peace, and of national honour. The confidence which the western people reposed in the government and their representatives is rewarded with success. They are reinstated in their rights with the least possible loss of time; and their harmony with the people of New Orleans, so necessary to the prosperity of the United States, which would have been broken, and the seeds of discord sown in its place, had hostilities been preferred to accommodation, remains unimpaired. Have the Federal ministers of the church meditated on these matters? and laying aside, as they ought to do, their electioneering and vindictive prayers and sermons, returned thanks that peace is preserved, and commerce, without the stain of blood?

In the pleasing contemplation of this state of things the mind, by comparison, carries itself back to those days of uproar and extravagance that marked the career of the former administration, and decides, by the unstudied impulse of its own feelings, that something must then have been wrong. Why was it, that America, formed for happiness, and remote by situation and circumstances from the troubles and tumults of the European world, became plunged into its vortex and contaminated with its crimes?

The answer is easy. Those who were then at the head of affairs were apostates from the principles of the revolution. Raised to an elevation they had not a right to expect, nor judgment to conduct, they became like feathers in the air, and blown about by every puff of passion or conceit.

Candour would find some apology for their conduct if want of judgment was their only defect. But error and crime, though often alike in their features, are distant in their characters and in their origin. The one has its source in the weakness of the head, the other in the hardness of the heart, and the coalition of the two, describes the former Administration.

Had no injurious consequences arisen from the conduct of that Administration, it might have passed for error or imbecility, and been permitted to die and be forgotten. The grave is kind to innocent offence. But even innocence, when it is a cause of injury, ought to undergo an enquiry.

The country, during the time of the former Administration, was kept in continual agitation and alarm; and that no investigation might be made into its conduct, it entrenched itself within a magic circle of terror, and called it a "sedition law." Violent and mysterious in its measures and arrogant in its manners, it affected to disdain information, and insulted the principles that raised it from obscurity.

John Adams and Timothy Pickering were men whom nothing but the accidents of the times rendered visible on the political horizon. Elevation turned their heads, and public indignation hath cast them to the ground. But an inquiry into the conduct and measures of that Administration is nevertheless necessary.

The country was put to great expense. Loans, taxes, and standing

41 | Letters to the Citizens of the United States

armies became the standing order of the day. The militia, said Secretary Pickering, are not to be depended upon, and fifty thousand men must be raised. For what? No cause to justify such measures has yet appeared. No discovery of such a cause has yet been made. The pretended Sedition Law shut up the sources of investigation, and the precipitate flight of John Adams closed the scene. But the matter ought not to sleep here.

It is not to gratify resentment, or encourage it in others, that I enter upon this subject. It is not in the power of man to accuse me of a persecuting spirit. But some explanation ought to be had. The motives and objects respecting the extraordinary and expensive measures of the former Administration ought to be known. The Sedition Law, that shield of the moment, prevented it then, and justice demands it now.

If the public have been imposed upon, it is proper they should know it; for where judgment is to act, or a choice is to be made, knowledge is first necessary. The conciliation of parties, if it does not grow out of explanation, partakes of the character of collusion or indifference.

There has been guilt somewhere; and it is better to fix it where it belongs, and separate the deceiver from the deceived, than that suspicion, the bane of society, should range at large, and sour the public mind. The military measures that were proposed and carrying on during the former administration, could not have for their object the defence of the country against invasion. This is a case that decides itself; for it is self evident, that while the war raged in Europe, neither France nor England could spare a man to send to America.

The object, therefore, must be something at home, and that something was the overthrow of the representative system of government, for it could be nothing else. But the plotters got into confusion and became enemies to each other. Adams hated and was jealous of Hamilton, and Hamilton hated and despised both Adams and Washington. Surly Timothy stood aloof, as he did at the affair of Lexington, and the part that fell to the public was to pay the expense.

But ought a people who, but a few years ago, were fighting the battles of the world, for liberty had no home but here, ought such a people to stand quietly by and see that liberty undermined by apostacy and overthrown by intrigue? Let the tombs of the slain recall their recollection, and the forethought of what their children are to be revive and fix in their hearts the love of liberty.

If the former administration can justify its conduct, give it the opportunity. The manner in which John Adams disappeared from the government renders an inquiry the more necessary. He gave some account of himself, lame and confused as it was, to certain *eastern wise men* who came to pay homage to him on his birthday. But if he thought it necessary to do this, ought he not to have rendered an account to the public. They had a right to expect it of him.

In that *tête-à-tête* account, he says, "Some measures were the effect of imperious necessity, much against my inclination." What measures does Mr. Adams mean, and what is the imperious necessity to which he alludes? "Others (says he) were measures of the Legislature, which, although approved when passed, were never previously proposed or recommended by me." What measures, it may be asked, were those, for the public have a right to know the conduct of their representatives? "Some (says he) left to my discretion were never executed, because no necessity for them, in my judgment, ever occurred."

What does this dark apology, mixed with accusation, amount to, but to increase and confirm the suspicion that something was wrong? Administration only was possessed of foreign official information, and it was only upon that information communicated by him publicly or privately, or to Congress, that Congress could act; and it is not in the power of Mr. Adams to show, from the condition of the belligerent powers, that any imperious necessity called for the warlike and expensive measures of his Administration.

What the correspondence between Administration and Rufus King in London, or Quincy Adams in Holland, or Berlin, might be, is but little known. The public papers have told us that the former became cup-bearer from the London underwriters to Captain Truxtun, for which, as Minister from a neutral nation, he ought to have been censured. It is, however, a feature that marks the politics of the Minister, and hints at the character of the correspondence.

I know that it is the opinion of several members of both houses of Congress, that an enquiry, with respect to the conduct of the late Administration, ought to be gone into. The convulsed state into which the country has been thrown will be best settled by a full and fair exposition of the conduct of that Administration, and the causes and object of that conduct. To be deceived, or to remain deceived, can be the interest of no man who seeks the public good; and it is the deceiver only, or one interested in the deception, that can wish to preclude enquiry.

The suspicion against the late Administration is, that it was plotting to overturn the representative system of government, and that it spread alarms of invasions that had no foundation, as a pretence for raising and establishing a military force as the means of accomplishing that object.

The law, called the Sedition Law, enacted, that if any person should write or publish, or cause to be written or published, any libel [without defining what a libel is] against the Government of the United States, or either house of congress, or against the President, he should be punished by a fine not exceeding two thousand dollars, and by imprisonment not exceeding two years.

But it is a much greater crime for a president to plot against a Constitution and the liberties of the people, than for an individual to plot against a President; and consequently, John Adams is accountable to the public for his conduct, as the individuals under his administration were to the sedition law.

The object, however, of an enquiry, in this case, is not to punish, but to satisfy; and to shew, by example, to future administrations, that an abuse of power and trust, however disguised by appearances, or rendered plausible by pretence, is one time or other to be accounted for.

Thomas Paine.
Bordentown, on the Delaware, New Jersey, March 12, 1803.

VII.

from the Trenton *True-American*, April 1803

The malignant mind, like the jaundiced eye, sees everything through a false medium of its own creating. The light of heaven appears stained with yellow to the distempered sight of the one, and the fairest actions have the form of crimes in the venomed imagination of the other.

For seven months, both before and after my return to America in October last, the apostate papers styling themselves "Federal" were filled with paragraphs and Essays respecting a letter from Mr. Jefferson to me at Paris; and though none of them knew the contents of the letter, nor the occasion of writing it, malignity taught them to suppose it, and the lying tongue of injustice lent them its aid.

That the public may no longer be imposed upon by Federal apostacy, I will now publish the Letter, and the occasion of its being written.

The Treaty negociated in England by John Jay, and ratified by the Washington Administration, had so disgracefully surrendered the right and freedom of the American flag, that all the Commerce of the United States on the Ocean became exposed to capture, and suffered in consequence of it. The duration of the Treaty was limited to two years after the war; and consequently America could not, during that period, relieve herself from the Chains which the Treaty had fixed upon her. This being the case, the only relief that could come must arise out of something originating in Europe, that would, in its consequences, extend to America. It had long been my opinion that Commerce contained within itself the means of its own protection; but as the time for bringing forward any new system is not always happening, it is necessary to watch its approach, and lay hold of it before it passes away.

As soon as the late Emperor Paul of Russia abandoned his coalition with England and become a Neutral Power, this crisis of time, and also of circumstances, was then arriving; and I employed it in arranging a plan for the protection of the Commerce of Neutral Nations during War, that might, in its operation and consequences, relieve the Commerce of America. The Plan, with the pieces accompanying it, consisted of about forty pages. The Citizen Bonneville, with whom I lived in Paris, translated it into French; Mr. Skipwith, the American Consul, Joel Barlow, and myself, had the translation printed and distributed as a present to the Foreign Ministers of all the Neutral Nations then resident in Paris. This was in the summer of 1800.

It was entitled Maritime Compact (in French *Pacte Maritime*). The plan, exclusive of the pieces that accompanied it, consisted of the following Preamble and Articles:

MARITIME COMPACT.

Being an Unarmed Association of Nations for the protection of the Rights and Commerce of Nations that shall be neutral in time of War.

Whereas, the Vexations and Injuries to which the Rights and Commerce of Neutral Nations have been, and continue to be, exposed during the time of maritime War, render it necessary to establish a law of Nations for the purpose of putting an end to such vexations and Injuries, and to guarantee to the Neutral Nations the exercise of their just Rights,

We, therefore, the undersigned Powers, form ourselves into an Association, and establish the following as a Law of Nations on the Seas.

ARTICLE THE FIRST.

Definition of the Rights of neutral Nations.

The Rights of Nations, such as are exercised by them in their intercourse with each other in time of Peace, are, and of right ought to be, the Rights of Neutral Nations at all times; because,

First, those Rights not having been abandoned by them, remain with them.

Secondly, because those Rights cannot become forfeited or void, in consequence of War breaking out between two or more other Nations.

A War of Nation against Nation being exclusively the act of the Nations that make the War, and not the act of the Neutral Nations, cannot, whether considered in itself or in its consequences, destroy or diminish the Rights of the Nations remaining in Peace.

ARTICLE THE SECOND.

The Ships and Vessels of Nations that rest neuter and at Peace with the World during a War with other Nations, have a Right to navigate freely on the Seas as they navigated before that War broke out, and to proceed to and enter the Port or Ports of any of the

Belligerent Powers, with the consent of that Power, without being seized, searched, visited, or any ways interrupted, by the Nation or Nations with which that Nation is at War.

ARTICLE THE THIRD.

For the Conservation of the aforesaid Rights, We, the undersigned Powers, engaging to each other our Sacred Faith and Honour, DECLARE

That if any Belligerent Power shall seize, search, visit, or any ways interrupt any Ship or Vessel belonging to the Citizens or Subjects of any of the Powers composing this Association, then each and all of the said undersigned Powers will cease to import, and will not permit to be imported into the Ports or Dominions of any of the said undersigned Powers, in any Ship or Vessel whatever, any Goods, wares, or Merchandize, produced or manufactured in, or exported from, the Dominions of the Power so offending against the Association hereby established and Proclaimed.

ARTICLE THE FOURTH.

That all the Ports appertaining to any and all of the Powers composing this Association shall be shut against the Flag of the offending Nation.

ARTICLE THE FIFTH.

That no remittance or payment in Money, Merchandize, or Bills of Exchange, shall be made by any of the Citizens, or Subjects, of any of the Powers composing this Association, to the Citizens or

Subjects of the offending Nation, for the Term of one year, or until reparation be made. The reparation to be — — times the amount of the damages sustained.

ARTICLE THE SIXTH.

If any Ship or Vessel appertaining to any of the Citizens or Subjects of any of the Powers composing this Association shall be seized, searched, visited, or interrupted, by any Belligerent Nation, or be forcibly prevented entering the Port of her destination, or be seized, searched, visited, or interrupted, in coming out of such Port, or be forcibly prevented from proceeding to any new destination, or be insulted or visited by any Agent from on board any Vessel of any Belligerent Power, the Government or Executive Power of the Nation to which the Ship or Vessel so seized, searched, visited, or interrupted belongs, shall, on evidence of the fact, make public Proclamation of the same, and send a Copy thereof to the Government, or Executive, of each of the Powers composing this Association, who shall publish the same in all the extent of his Dominions, together with a Declaration, that at the expiration of — — days after publication, the penal articles of this Association shall be put in execution against the offending Nation.

ARTICLE THE SEVENTH.

If reparation be not made within the space of one year, the said Proclamation shall be renewed for one year more, and so on.

ARTICLE THE EIGHTH.

The Association chooses for itself a Flag to be carried at the

Mast-head conjointly with the National Flag of each Nation composing this Association.

The Flag of the Association shall be composed of the same colors as compose the Rain-bow, and arranged in the same order as they appear in that Phenomenon.

ARTICLE THE NINTH.

And whereas, it may happen that one or more of the Nations composing this Association may be, at the time of forming it, engaged in War or become so in future, in that case, the Ships and Vessels of such Nation shall carry the Flag of the Association bound round the Mast, to denote that the Nation to which she belongs is a Member of the Association and a respecter of its Laws.

N. B. This distinction in the manner of carrying the Flag is mearly for the purpose, that Neutral Vessels having the Flag at the Mast-head, may be known at first sight.

ARTICLE THE TENTH.

And whereas, it is contrary to the moral principles of Neutrality and Peace, that any Neutral Nation should furnish to the Belligerent Powers, or any of them, the means of carrying on War against each other, We, therefore, the Powers composing this Association, Declare, that we will each one for itself, prohibit in our Dominions the exportation or transportation of military stores, comprehending gunpowder, cannon, and cannon-balls, fire arms of all kinds, and all kinds of iron and steel weapons used in War. Excluding therefrom all kinds of Utensils and Instruments used in civil or domestic life, and every other article that cannot, in its immediate state, be employed in War.

Having thus declared the moral Motives of the foregoing Article,

51 | Letters to the Citizens of the United States

We declare also the civil and political Intention thereof, to wit,

That as Belligerent Nations have no right to visit or search any Ship or Vessel belonging to a Nation at Peace, and under the protection of the Laws and Government thereof, and as all such visit or search is an insult to the Nation to which such Ship or Vessel belongs and to the Government of the same, We, therefore, the Powers composing this Association, will take the right of prohibition on ourselves to whom it properly belongs, and by whom only it can be legally exercised, and not permit foreign Nations, in a state of War, to usurp the right of legislating by Proclamation for any of the Citizens or Subjects of the Powers composing this Association.

It is, therefore, in order to take away all pretence of search or visit, which by being offensive might become a new cause of War, that we will provide Laws and publish them by Proclamation, each in his own Dominion, to prohibit the supplying, or carrying to, the Belligerent Powers, or either of them, the military stores or articles before mentioned, annexing thereto a penalty to be levied or inflicted upon any persons within our several Dominions transgressing the same. And we invite all Persons, as well of the Belligerent Nations as of our own, or of any other, to give information of any knowledge they may have of any transgressions against the said Law, that the offenders may be prosecuted.

By this conduct we restore the word Contraband (contra and ban) to its true and original signification, which means against Law, edict, or Proclamation; and none but the Government of a Nation can have, or can exercise, the right of making Laws, edicts, or Proclamations, for the conduct of its Citizens or Subjects.

Now We, the undersigned Powers, declare the aforesaid Articles to be a Law of Nations at all times, or until a Congress of Nations shall meet to form some Law more effectual.

And we do recommend that immediately on the breaking out of War between any two or more Nations, that Deputies be appointed by all Neutral Nations, whether members of this Association or not, to meet in Congress in some central place to take cognizance of any violations of the Rights of Neutral Nations.

Signed, &c.

For the purpose of giving operation to the aforesaid plan of an *unarmed Association,* the following Paragraph was subjoined:

"It may be judged proper for the order of Business, that the Association of Nations have a President for a term of years, and the Presidency to pass by rotation, to each of the parties composing the Association.

"In that case, and for the sake of regularity, the first President to be the Executive power of the most northerly Nation composing the Association, and his deputy or Minister at the Congress to be President of the Congress, — and the next most northerly to be Vice-president, who shall succeed to the Presidency, and so on. The line determining the Geographical situation of each, to be the latitude of the Capital of each Nation.

"If this method be adopted it will be proper that the first President be nominally constituted in order to give rotation to the rest. In that case the following Article might be added to the foregoing, viz't. The Constitution of the Association nominates the Emperor Paul to be *first President* of the Association of Nations for the protection of Neutral Commerce, and securing the freedom of the Seas."

The foregoing plan, as I have before mentioned, was presented to the Ministers of all the Neutral Nations then in Paris, in the summer of 1800. Six Copies were given to the Russian General Springporten;

53 | Letters to the Citizens of the United States

and a Russian Gentleman who was going to Petersburgh took two expressly for the purpose of putting them into the hands of Paul. I sent the original manuscript, in my own handwriting, to Mr. Jefferson, and also wrote him four Letters, dated the 1st, 4th, 6th, 16th of October, 1800, giving him an account of what was then going on in Europe respecting Neutral Commerce.

The Case was, that in order to compel the English Government to acknowledge the rights of Neutral Commerce, and that free Ships make free Goods, the *Emperor Paul,* in the month of September following the publication of the plan, shut all the Ports of Russia against England. Sweden and Denmark did the same by their Ports, and Denmark shut up Hamburgh. Prussia shut up the Elbe and the Weser.

The ports of Spain, Portugal, and Naples were shut up, and, in general, all the ports of Italy, except Venice, which the Emperor of Germany held; and had it not been for the untimely death of *Paul, a Law of Nations,* founded on the authority of Nations, for establishing the rights of Neutral Commerce and the freedom of the Seas, would have been proclaimed, and the Government of England must have consented to that Law, or the Nation must have lost its Commerce; and the consequence to America would have been, that such a Law would, in a great measure if not entirely, have released her from the injuries of Jay's Treaty.

Of all these matters I informed Mr. Jefferson. This was before he was President, and the Letter he wrote me after he was President was in answer to those I had written to him and the manuscript Copy of the plan I had sent here. Here follows the Letter:

Washington, March 18, 1801.

Dear Sir:
Your letters of Oct. 1st, 4th, 6th, 16th, came duly to hand,

and the papers which they covered were, according to your permission, published in the Newspapers, and in a Pamphlet, and under your own name. These papers contain precisely our principles, and I hope they will be generally recognized here. *Determined as we are to avoid, if possible, wasting the energies of our People in war and destruction, we shall avoid implicating ourselves with the Powers of Europe, even in support of principles which we mean to pursue. They have so many other Interests different from ours that we must avoid being entangled in them. We believe we can enforce those principles as to ourselves by Peaceable means, now that we are likely to have our Public Councils detached from foreign views.* The return of our citizens from the phrenzy into which they had been wrought, partly by ill conduct in France, partly by artifices practiced upon them, is almost extinct, and will, I believe, become quite so. But these details, too minute and long for a Letter, will be better developed by Mr. Dawson, the Bearer of this, a Member of the late Congress, to whom I refer you for them. He goes in the *Maryland,* Sloop of War, which will wait a few days at Havre to receive his Letters to be written on his arrival at Paris. You expressed a wish to get a passage to this Country in a Public Vessel. Mr. Dawson is charged with orders to the Captain of the *Maryland* to receive and accommodate you back if you can be ready to depart at such a short warning. Rob't R. Livingston is appointed Minister Plenipotentiary to the Republic of France, but will not leave this, till we receive the ratification of the Convention by Mr. Dawson. I am in hopes you will find us returned generally to sentiments worthy of former times. In these it will be your glory to have steadily laboured and with as much effect as any man living. That you may long live to continue your useful Labours and to reap the reward in the thankfulness of Nations is my sincere prayer. Accept assurances of my high esteem and affectionate attachment.

ThomasJefferson.

This, Citizens of the United States, is the Letter about which the leaders and tools of the Federal faction, without knowing its contents or the occasion of writing it, have wasted so many malignant falsehoods.

It is a Letter which, on account of its wise economy and peaceable principles, and its forbearance to reproach, will be read by every good Man and every good Citizen with pleasure; and the faction, mortified at its appearance, will have to regret they forced it into publication. The least atonement they can now offer is to make the Letter as public as they have made their own infamy, and learn to lie no more.

The same injustice they shewed to Mr. Jefferson they shewed to me. I had employed myself in Europe, and at my own expense, in forming and promoting a plan that would, in its operation, have benefited the Commerce of America; and the faction here invented and circulated an account in the papers they employ, that I had given a plan to the French for burning all the towns on the Coast from Savannah to Baltimore.

Were I to prosecute them for this (and I do not promise that I will not, for the Liberty of the Press is not the liberty of lying,) there is not a fæderal judge, not even one of Midnight appointment, but must, from the nature of the case, be obliged to condemn them. The faction, however, cannot complain they have been restrained in any thing. They have had their full swing of lying uncontradicted; they have availed themselves, unopposed, of all the arts Hypocrisy could devise; and the event has been, what in all such cases it ever will and ought to be, the *ruin of themselves*.

The Characters of the late and of the present Administrations are now sufficiently marked, and the adherents of each keep up the distinction. The former Administration rendered itself notorious by outrage, coxcombical parade, false alarms, a continued increase of taxes, and an unceasing clamor for War; and as every vice has a virtue opposed to it, the present Administration moves on the direct contrary line. The question, therefore, at elections is not properly a question upon Persons, but upon principles. Those who are for Peace, moderate taxes, and mild Government, will vote for the Administration that conducts itself by those principles, in whatever hands that Administration may be.

There are in the United States, and particularly in the middle States, several religious Sects, whose leading moral principle is *peace*. It is, therefore, impossible that such Persons, consistently with the dictates of that principle, can vote for an Administration that is clamorous for War. When moral principles, rather than Persons, are candidates for Power, to vote is to perform a moral duty, and not to vote is to neglect a duty.

That persons who are hunting after places, offices, and contracts, should be advocates for War, taxes, and extravagance, is not to be wondered at; but that so large a portion of the People who had nothing to depend upon but their Industry, and no other public prospect but that of paying taxes, and bearing the burden, should be advocates for the same measures, is a thoughtlessness not easily accounted for. But reason is recovering her empire, and the fog of delusion is clearing away.

Thomas Paine.

Bordentown, on the Delaware, New Jersey, April 21, 1803.

VIII.

from the Philadelphia *Aurora*, June 7, 1805

Much has been said, and much remains to be said, of that undescribed and undescribable *nothing,* called federalism. It is a word without a meaning, and designates a faction that has no principles. Ask a man who called himself a federalist, what federalism is, and he cannot tell you. Ask him, what are its principles, and he has none to give. Federalism, then, with respect to government, is similar to atheism with respect to religion, a *nominal nothing* without principles. The federal papers, especially those of New England, have often said, that *"religion and federalism must go together."* But if their religion is related to their federalism; if it is as destitute of morals as their federalism is of principles; and I fear it is; it will do them no good in this world or the next. It will condemn them as imposters and hypocrites in both.

Those who once figured as leaders under the assumed and fraudulent name of *federalism* (but who are since gone, not into honorable and peaceable retirement, like *John Dickinson* and *Charles Thomson* but into obscurity and oblivion, like John Adams and John Jay), had some plans in contemplation which they concealed from their deluded adherents, but those plans can be discovered through the gauzy, but clumsy, veil of conduct those leaders adopted. *"No cover is large enough to hide itself"* says the Spanish proverb.

It requires more artifice and management to disguise and conceal sinister designs than schemers are aware of. A man never turns a rogue but he turns a fool. He incautiously lets out something by which those he intended to cheat or impose upon begin to *find him out*. Whereas truth is a straight forward thing, even an ignorant man will not blunder in a true story — nor can an artful man keep a false story straight.

But those leaders, supposing themselves in a higher position than what common observation would reach, presume, on their supposed consequence and the expected credulity of their adherents, to impose on the nation by clamorous and false pretences, for the purpose of raising a standing army of fifty thousand men; and when they had got that army the mask would have been thrown off, and their deluded adherents would have paid the price of their duplicity by being enslaved.

But in the midst of this career of delusion and imposition, those leaders became fools. They did everything they ought not to have done. They advocated plans which showed that their intention and their cause were not good. They labored to provoke war. They opposed every thing which led to peace. They loaded the country with vexatious and unnecessary taxes, and then opposed the reduction of them. They opposed a reduction of useless offices that served no other purpose than to maintain their own partisans at the expense of the public. In short, they run themselves a-ground first, by their extravagance and next by their folly. Blinded by their own vanity, and though bewildered in the wilderness of their own projects, they foolishly supposed themselves above detection. They had neither sense enough to know, nor logic enough to perceive, that as we can reason upward from cause to effect, so also can we reason downward from effect to cause, and discover, by the means they make use of, the motives and object of any party; for when the means are bad, the motive and the end to be obtained cannot be good.

The manners also, and language of any party is another clue that leads to a discovery of their real characters. When the cause and principles of a party are *good,* its advocates make use of *reason, argument,* and *good language. Truth* can derive no advantage from boisterous *vulgarity.* But when the motives and principles of a party are *bad,* it is necessary to *conceal them;* and its abettors having *principles they dare to acknowledge* and cannot *defend,* avoid everything of argument, and take refuge in *abuse* and *falsehood.*

The federal papers are an instance of the justness of this remark. Their pages are crowded with abuse, but never with argument; for they have no principles to argue from: and as to falsehood, it is become so naturally their *mother tongue,* especially in New England, that they seem to have lost the *power* as well as the *disposition,* of speaking the *truth.* Those papers have been of great aid to the republican cause, not only by the additional disgrace they have brought on their own disgraceful faction, but by serving as a foil to set off, with greater eclat, the decency and well principled arguments of the republican papers. I have had some experience, perhaps as much as most men have had in the various turns of political life, but I never saw a greater set of fools undertake to conduct a party than the leaders of the federalists have been, and the editors of their papers. They correspond to the story told of a man who was become so proud and famous for lying that he disdained speaking truth lest he should lose his character.

Cannot those stupid people see, or, according to some dogmas, of their own, are their hearts hardened, that they shall not see, that the more vulgar and abusive they are, the more ground they lose in the estimation of the public. Every election, especially in New England, is wearing them down, till they will be lost even as a faction, and Massachusetts and Connecticut will recover their former character. Everything this faction does hastens its exit. The abusive vulgarity of Hulbert, a pettyfogging attorney of Sheffield, in Massachusetts, and one of its legislators, has contributed to bring forward the funeral. In his late unprincipled speech in the legislature of that state, he has driven another nail in the coffin of the federal faction, and I leave to the *New England* Palladium to clinch it. It is a paper worthy of being the buffoon of such a faction, and of such an hypocritical impostor — Thus much for the character of parties and the method of ascertaining their motives and objects. I now proceed to other matters.

When I returned to America in November 1802 (after an absence of more than fourteen years) I found the country in a state of disquietude. The people were divided into two classes, under the names of *republicans* and *federalists,* and in point of numbers appeared to be nearly balanced. The republicans were the majority in congress, and all the administration were of that description; but they were assailed with outrageous abuse in the federal papers, but never by argument. I am enough acquainted with life and the world, to know, that *abuse* is the evidence of *want of argument,* and that those who use it, have no right on their side. There is a dignified calmness in conscious rectitude, which descends not to abuse. It can reason but it cannot rage. It cannot quit the strong fortress of rectitude to skirmish in the fields of vulgarity.

It was not difficult to perceive, that this division and agitation arose from some reports spread during the administration of John Adams, and in the latter time of General Washington, which one part of the people believed, and the other did not; and the point to be ascertained was whether those reports were true or false. If either of those cases could be ascertained effectually, it would unite the people. The chief of those reports, was the danger of an *invasion* from France; and this was made a cause for borrowing, by loan, at the high rate of *eight per cent,* laying on a land tax of two million dollars annually; besides a greater number of other taxes; and for raising a standing army of fifty thousand men.

Now, if the danger was real, it ought to have been provided against. If it was a fiction, with the design of raising an army to be employed to accomplish some concealed purpose, the country ought to be informed of it. The party styling themselves federalists appeared to believe the danger, and the republicans to ridicule it as fabulous; and in this state the parties stood. It was, however, equally the interest of both to know the truth, on which ever side the truth might fall.

Being at Washington in the winter of 1802-3, I talked with some members of congress on the subject, particularly with Mr. Breckenridge, senator from Kentucky, the same person who brought in the bill for repealing John Adams's judiciary law, and the midnight appointments made in the consequence of it. This repeal saved the country *thirty-two thousand dollars annually,* besides freeing it from an intended judiciary despotism.

I spoke to him of the propriety of congress appointing a committee, or by some other method as they might think proper, to enquire into the conduct of the former administration, that of John Adams, and to call upon him to produce the information whether official or otherwise, which he went upon, if he had any, for putting the country to such vast expence, under the idea, real or pretended, of an invasion from France. This would be giving John Adams a fair chance of clearing himself, if he could, from the suspicion that his administration was a gross imposition on the public; and on the other hand, if the imposition should be proved, it would enlighten the country, and put it on its guard against future impositions.

Mr. Breckenridge agreed with me in the propriety and fitness of the measure. He saw that information was wanted, and that it would be useful, because when the truth should be known, it would compose the people. John Adams had gone away in what may be called a *clandestine manner,* without surrendering into the hands of his successor, as he ought to have done in person, any account of the affairs of the executive department, foreign or domestic. There are no papers or documents that I know of, and I believe there are none, because there can be none in the secretary of state's office, that will justify John Adams in the expence to which his administration put the country; or even afford ground for suspicion that either France or England intended to invade the United States. For what purpose then was an army to be raised. The projectors of such a measure must have had some object in view, and as that object has never been explained, it ought to be enquired into. It is bad policy, and also a bad precedent, expecially in public affairs, to let imposition slide away without detection.

At the time I talked with Mr. Breckenridge on this subject, I expected that Mr. *Skipwith* formerly and at this time, American consul at Paris, and *Joel Barlow* would soon arrive, and I did not wish the enquiry to be gone into till they came. After the fall of Robespierre and the establishment of the directory constitution, these two gentlemen and myself (Mr. Monroe being recalled) had better opportunities of knowing the sentiments and intentions of the French government with respect to American than other persons had; and they can be evidence equally with myself, that no intention existed in the French government to invade America; nor was any preparation made for such an attempt, nor could it be made. The possibility of such a thing did not exist. The French navy at that time was nearly annihilated; her ports blockaded by the British; and she had to fight by land, single handed, against almost the whole of Europe. She had it not in her power to spare a

63 | Letters to the Citizens of the United States

regiment, much less could she spare an *army,* to send to America; and if she could have spared one, she had not the means of transporting it, nor the convoy to protect it. All the circumstances as well as the evidence that can be provided, will show that the administration of John Adams was a fraudulent and expensive imposition on the country; and that the army to be raised was intended for some secret purpose, and not for the purpose of defence. If John Adams was not conscious of something wrong, and apprehensive of some consequences, why did he abscond in the hasty and private manner he did? or why did his partisans want to put Aaron Burr in the presidency. In the days of the black cockades John Adams had one so enormous and so valiantly large, that he appeared to be suspended by it; but when his *midnight hour* arrived, his valor fled and himself also.

The *voluntary embassy* of Dr. Logan to Paris appears to have disconcerted John's administration, and discomfited its leaders; because it served to expose and put an end to their projects. When Dr. Logan called on Timothy Pickering, secretary of state, with Mr. Skipwith's dispatches from Paris, Timothy, before he knew their contents, though Logan knew the whole, began to talk of invasions and dangers, and the necessity of *preparation.* "It may be very well" said Logan, "to have the militia in good order." "The militia, sir!"

said Timothy, *"the militia never did any good and never will.*[1] *We must have any army of fifty thousand men."* When Logan was coming away, Timothy said to him at the door, "Sir, the government don't thank you."

When Logan waited on General Washington, who had been then appointed lieutenant general of the army then raising, of which John was commander in chief! — the General received him coldly and sternly, and said to him in a haughty tone, *"and pray sir, what right have you, that are but a private citizen, to interfere in matters of government?"* Logan very prudently replied, "I have no answer, sir, to make to that," and withdrew. The state of Pennsylvania, soon after this, elected Dr. Logan one of its senators in congress.

Circumstances often unriddle and explain *themselves,* and it happens so in this case; for if the administration, and those leaders connected with it, were sincere in their belief that the danger was real, and that the country (as *Gouverneur Morris* expressed it, in his *funeral* oration on Hamilton) was *"menaced with dangers from without,"* and that France intended an invasion; and if, at the same

---

[1] Timothy Pickering's reflection on the *militia* deserves a rebuff. It was the militia that fought at *Bunker's hill,* under *Warren,* a military general. It was by the aid of numerous reinforcements of militia to join General Gates that *Burgoyne* was taken. It was by a volunteer militia under *Starfl,* a volunteer general, that Col. *Baum,* a Hessian officer, was defeated at Bennington, in Vermont, which was the prelude to the capture of Burgoyne. But perhaps Timothy reasons from himself; and if he makes himself the standard by which to judge of the merits of the militia there is ground for his saying the *militia never did any good and never will.* Timothy's first public employment was very harmless, that of a teacher of psalmody. W{ien the revolution began he *learned* the *manual exercise,* and then *taught it.* He was afterwards appointed a colonel of a regiment of *militia,* and when the affairs of *Lexington and Concord* took place, April 19, 1775, and the British were retreating from Concord back to Boston, an order was sent to *Timothy,* to march with his regiment, and post himself at a certain place to cut off their retreat. Timothy marched but he stopped short of the *place,* and drew up his men, and went to prayers, till the British passed it. His prayers saved him from the *dangers* of that day. I do not know that he sung psalms. Perhaps not. The enemy might have *overheard him.* Had Timothy done his duty on that occasion, and put his trust in God without loitering away his time, the whole party of the British, about two thousand, must have been prisoners, for they could not have got back into Boston; and the slaughter at Bunker's hill, the 17th of June following, could not have taken place. The whole force of the British at Boston at that time was about four thousand; *one half* of which were on this expedition. — *Author.*

65 | Letters to the Citizens of the United States

time, they had no concealed object in contemplation themselves, they would welcome the messenger that should bring them good tidings that *all was well.* But if, on the contrary, they *new* they were acting a *fraud,* and heating the country with falsehoods and false alarms for the purpose of procuring loans, levying new taxes, and raising an army to accomplish some *concealed purpose* that could not be accomplished without that treachery, they would be *enraged at him;* and this accounts for the rude reception Dr. Logan received from that administration. Thousands who supported that administration from a belief that it was acting right, have since abandoned it from a conviction that it acted deceitfully wrong, and this also accounts for the great majority at the last presidential election. We have no alarms now, nor should we have had any then, if the present administration had existed at that time.

It requires only a prudent and honest administration to preserve America always in peace. Her distance from the European world frees her from its intrigues. But when men get into power, whose heads, like the head of *John Adams,* are filled with *"strange notions"* and counter revolutionary principles and projects, things will be sure to go wrong. John Adams, who was more the *dupe* of a party than the *leader* of it, entered on the office of president with his *head turned* by the *elevation* he was lifted to; and his principles (if ever he had any), corrupted. He turned out to be a counter revolutionist; and if the concealed objects of his administration had succeeded, the federal constitution would have been destroyed, and that by persons under the assumed and fraudulent name of *federalists.*

"As General Washington (said John Adams) *has no children, it will be right to make the government in the family of Lund Washington."* Perhaps John intended this as a sly introduction of himself and his hopeful son *Quincy,* in preference to any of the Washingtons; for this same John Adams was one of the *chiefs* of a party in *congress at*

Yorktown in Pennsylvania, in the latter end of the year 1777 and beginning of '78, for dismissing *Washington* from the command of the army, *because,* they said, *he was not capable of it and did nothing.* Yet under John's administration the name of Washington was made use of, for the purpose of introducing and covering a counter revolutionary system. Such is the inconsistency of faction and of men who have no fixed principles!

The independence of America would have added but little to her own happiness, and been of no benefit to the world, if her government had been formed on the *corrupt models of the old world.* It was the opportunity of *beginning the world anew,* as it were; and of bringing forward a *new system* of government in which the rights of *all* men should be preserved that gave *value* to independence. The pamphlet *Common Sense,* the first work I ever published, embraced both those objects. *Mere* independence might at some future time, have been effected and established by arms, *without principle,* but a *just* system of government could not. In short, it was the *principle,'* at *that* time, that produced the independence; for until the principle spread itself abroad among the people, independence was not thought of, and America was fighting without an object. Those who know the circumstances of the times I speak of, know this to be true.

I am not persecuting John Adams, nor any other man, nor did I ever persecute any; but I see the propriety, and even the necessity of instituting an enquiry into the confused state of affairs during his administration. All the circumstances and the evidence combined with them, justify the suspicion that during *that* administration the country was grossly imposed upon, and put to so great and unnecessary expence, which the present administration has to pay off; and that some concealed counter-revolutionary scheme was in contemplation. The leaders, separately, might hide from each other what his own particular object was. Each of them might have a *different one*. But all of them agreed in the preliminary project, that of raising an army: and the case would have been, that when they had collected that army, they would have broken into distinct parties, like the generals of Alexander's army, and destroyed each other, to decide who should be the reigning usurper. Symptoms of disgust had already begun to appear among the chiefs. Hamilton despised Washington; Adams was jealous of Hamilton; and Hamilton had a perfect contempt for Adams. But in the end, John, I believe would have come poorly off. He was not a man of the sword, but only of *the cockade*.

I purposely delayed entering upon this subject till the presidential election should be over. Had I published it before that time the clamor of faction would have said it was an electioneering trick. *Now,* they cannot say it. The choice made at that election was the spontaneous choice of the people, and is therefore the more honorable both to the electors and the elected. The country at this time, compared with what it was two or three years ago, is in a state of tranquility; and in a fit disposition of calmness to take the matters herein stated into consideration before the next meeting of congress. It is by keeping a country well informed upon its affairs, and discarding from its councils every thing of mystery, that harmony is preserved or restored among the people, and confidence reposed in the government.

Thomas Paine.

June 5th, 1805.

www.ingramcontent.com/pod-product-compliance
Lightning Source LLC
Chambersburg PA
CBHW030456010526
44118CB00011B/970